Buckaloose

Library of Congress Catalog Card Number: 2002109700

ISBN 1-56647-572-4

First Printing, October 2002

1 2 3 4 5 6 7 8 9

Design by Mardee Domingo Melton

Front cover: Photo of Israel Kamakawiwo'ole taken by Elizabeth and George Studios [Tropical Music, Inc.], and a view of Palolo Valley taken from the Kaimuki fire station [Bishop Museum].

Except where otherwise credited, all photographs in this book are taken from the author's private collection. Kaimuki Intermediate and High School Yearbooks courtesy of David Kuwada.

Mutual Publishing
1215 Center Street, Suite 210
Honolulu, Hawai'i 96816
Ph: (808) 732-1709
Fax: (808) 734-4094
e-mail: mutual@lava.net
www.mutualpublishing.com
Printed in Korea.

Buckaloose

KAIMUKI SCHOOL DAYS WITH ISRAEL KAMAKAWIWO'OLE

Sam Kong

Hanabatta Days

"Class! We're going to soon be getting a new student from Ni'ihau."

Back then we didn't know much about Ni'ihau. Our teacher added to its mystique, for she knew very little of that privately owned island. But by the time she finished telling us what it might be like to live on an isolated island, thoughts of old Hawai'i were not far from everyone's mind.

When Israel Kamakawiwo'ole walked into class that first day, he just looked like he could live and survive off the land on his own. Just think, a life without TV dinners... He shuffled over to his chair and sat down smiling, not saying a word. It wasn't that he seemed shy. More like, "He's got a secret that he doesn't want to tell yet" kind of attitude. Which was perfect because it made Ni'ihau and old Hawai'i even more mysterious.

It was a perfect time for Israel to show up at Wai'alae Elementary school... 1969... 4th grade... Hawaiian Studies... back in the days when slippers were optional.

You remember? How many times did you forget your slippers up at the park? Funny how you don't remember taking them off, but then, how else could you run? Basketball, and especially kickball, on the hot basketball courts, no problem. I used to hate when I returned to class from recess, and as soon as my feet hit the cold linoleum, oh no, forgot my slippers. Then, of course, the teacher would ask me where my slippers were, and all I could do was make a sad face and say, "Stay broke."

So we learned not to ask for li hing mui or lemon peel; it was a gift, and one doesn't ask for gifts.

This view of Kaimuki in the early '60s shows 9th Avenue as seen from Wai'alae Avenue. A great street for playing Sky Inning.

[Ray Jerome Baker/Bishop Museum]

Wai'alae looked a little different than it does now. The first thing you'd notice now is that Mr. Imai's house is gone. It was this little old house on the corner of 19th and Harding Ave, right on school property. Mr. Imai was the school's caretaker. He was quiet as he went about working around the school, and he liked us kids.

One day, Israel and I were walking in school, and as it just so happens, we were walking behind Mr. Imai. No big deal, you see him all the time. But this time he reaches into his pocket and drops some stuff, and keeps walking. So we picked it up, and it was homemade lemon peel! There were always jars sitting in the sun outside his house.

After that we used to just follow him around when we wanted something to snack on. Word got out, and one day as we were following Mr. Imai, some other kids just walked up to him and asked for some lemon peel, and he said, "No more." So they left, but Israel said, "Stay get." I believed him, and we kind of knew he had. Mr. Imai would have told us he didn't have before we started to follow him. So we didn't say a word, and kept following. Sure enough, he'd slip some packages out and drop them to the ground for Israel and me. Too cool. So we learned not to ask for li hing mui or lemon peel; it was a gift, and one doesn't ask for gifts.

In 5th grade the school announced Mr. Imai's retirement, and he was more shocked than anyone else at this news. See, he had no plans of retiring. They fixed it later on. It was actually a teacher that was retiring. Wai'alae Elementary without Mr. Imai, we couldn't imagine that.

Wai'alae Elementary with class pictures from 1965, 1966, 1967 and 1968. Say cheese!

1965

1966

1967

1968

10 Buckaloose

The other thing that is missing at Wai‘alae Elementary now is the 5th grade wooden building, which was right in the middle of the school. There's a field there now, where once stood a building that would remind you of Noah's Ark. This was really my favorite school building! We spent summers in there because we borrowed the classrooms for Summer Fun.

Summer Fun, that's when we had to bring home-lunch, and got to do all kinds of things—from the "Junior Olympics" to the weekly excursion. Did you ever get to go camping at Hanauma Bay? You want to know how mischievous our bruddah can be? Check this out. We were camping at Hanauma Bay for a summer fun excursion. The first morning, a few of us woke up early and were up and about, all excited. Israel was already up, and was down by the beach cruising. I started off towards Israel with a couple guys following behind. But when he saw us coming, he did something strange. As I got closer, Israel just kept smiling, but said to me, "No come." I immediately slowed my walk, but still kept moving towards him. As I got closer, he started looking more serious, and under his breath he said again, "No come." So I stopped. At that moment, our two friends walked past me, not really paying attention to Israel. He was smiling big again. As I stood there pondering what was happening, our two friends suddenly disappeared! Actually, they were face down in the sand. See, Israel had dug a wide hole and covered it with a towel, sprinkled with sand. I couldn't believe it. We just cracked up. Hey, I'm just glad it wasn't me. And you know, it was a good start to learn to listen…and trust.

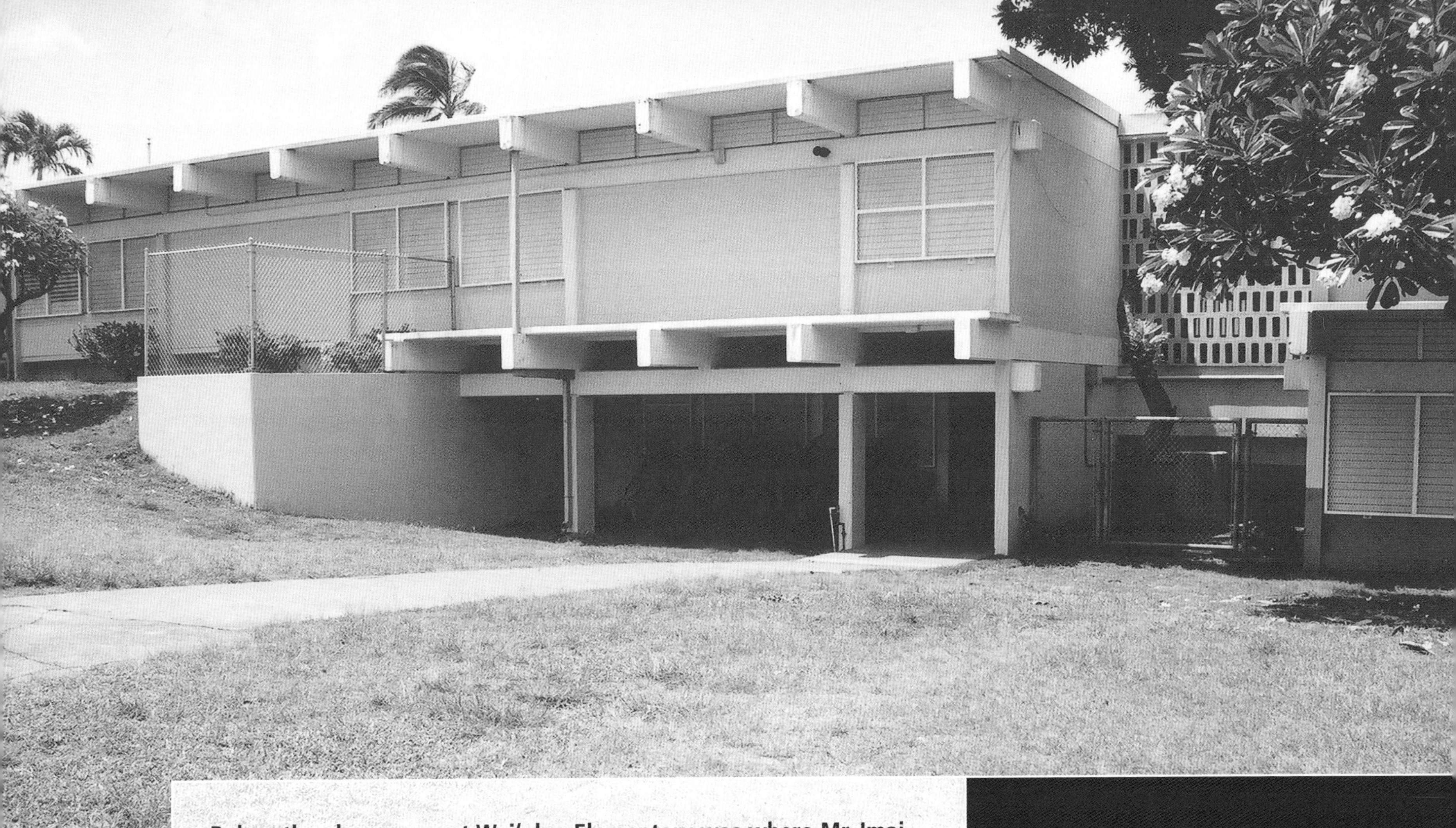

Below the classrooms at Wai'alae Elementary was where Mr. Imai, the school caretaker, kept his equipment and an endless supply of lemon peel and li hing mui for the kids.

...it was a good start to learn to listen...and trust.

Chase Master

A*ctually, I knew Israel* before he first stepped foot in class. Back in those days we had a big group of neighborhood kids. We all hung out together and our favorite thing was playing in yards and on the street—our noses in everybody's business. It just so happened, I lived only three houses from Petrie Park on 20th Avenue. Israel lived down a lane on 19th. The first time we met was right in front of his house. You've heard people talk about sitting under the mango tree. Well, Israel was doing just that. See, in front of his house there was a very tilted V-shaped mango tree. One of the trunks went straight up, and the other went sideways, so perfect for sitting. And that's where he was.

Petrie Park on 20th Avenue in Kaimuki was the best place for flying kites and letting them go "BUCKALOOSE!"

One day I made Skippy laugh so hard he was rolling on the ground.

Buckaloose

Funny, when you're a kid, you don't know what "ethnicity" or "nationality" means, so even if Israel was Hawaiian, who cared? All you knew is that you got one more friend to play with. And how many people can say they played Chase Master with Israel? Yes, he was big, even when we were little. But we played Chase Master and a lot of Sky Inning.

Sometimes Israel's brother, Skippy, would come out and watch us play. One day I made Skippy laugh so hard he was rolling on the ground. Skippy was sitting on the mango tree, watching us play Chase Master. I kind of used the tree and Skippy as a screen, and yes, Skippy was big too. I tried to make a quick get-away from the others by ducking under the branch Skippy was sitting on, but I misjudged. As I whacked my forehead on the branch, my feet kept going forward. So as you can imagine, in a split second I was flat on my back, so fast that I wasn't too sure what had happened. But as I lay there, I could hear Skippy cracking up above my head. You know, of course, everyone else joined in on the laughter… no one asked me if I was all right…

Everyone got to be "it" at some point while playing Chase Master. [Kaimuki Intermediate School Yearbook]

If you were to watch us play Chase Master, you'd notice something right off. First, Israel wasn't always "it." Well, everyone got to be "it" sometimes, but no one picked on anyone in particular. We didn't play that way. Second, you'd notice that sooner or later, Israel was going to drop out. At some point while we were playing, we'd stop and realize that Israel was missing. "Where's Israel?" someone would ask, and we would then notice Israel sitting down on the side. The first time we asked him what was up, all he said was, "Tired." So then we, too, would just sit down, cruise, talk story…

Kahala Mall and Flying Kites

O*ne day, since he was the "new guy"* in the neighborhood, we asked him what he wanted to do. All he said was "Kahala Mall." So we started walking down the street. Going to Kahala Mall was no big deal, even though we were kind of young. I used to go down by myself as far back as I can remember, most times with a specific destination…to the barber shop to get my famous crew cut. It's hard for me to believe that crew cuts are stylish now. Anyway, the Mall wasn't even enclosed back then, and it still had corrugated roofing. Our favorite store had to be Woolworths. The aroma of hotdogs! Not to mention their cone sushi and fried chicken!

Woolworths at Kahala Mall had the best cone sushi and fried chicken. [Hawai'i State Archives]

When it came to food, sharing really was a way of life for us.

On the way down, I asked him what Ni‘ihau was like. His reply was, “Same thing, but no more Kahala Mall.” That was it. At that age, I really wasn’t expecting some inside revelation on the mysteries of Ni‘ihau, but all I got was, “Same thing, but no more Kahala Mall.”

When we got to Kahala Mall we made our intricate plans to grind. See, Longs used to have a soda machine in the store. The kind that dispenses a cup, then ice, then the soda. But as mentioned, Woolworths had the cone sushi and fried chicken. So we would split up, making sure we had enough money, do our assigned duties, and meet back with the “community food” to be shared by all. You know you can’t really break up a cone sushi. You have to share bites. When it came to food, sharing really was a way of life for us.

Anyway, Israel really had an attraction to the Mall. He always wanted to go there to cruise. I guess it was like a new thing for him. For me, it usually just meant another haircut. He had that same attraction to Waikiki later on.

At Kahala Mall, other than food, we probably bought more kites than anything else. Remember how popular it was to fly those diamond-shape kites? At Woolworths and at Longs, the large one was only 25 cents, and the smaller one was 17 cents. Would you believe, Israel flew each kite only once? We would walk down to the Mall after school, buy the kite, return home to build it, and head to Petrie Park. I used to like the 1000-foot roll of string, but sometimes we had to make due with the 250-foot rolls.

At first, we would just work our kites up and out, but there's always that point of "no return." Not that it mattered. That's when the excitement started. You never knew which kite would be the first to buckaloose. Sometimes our kites would be over Diamond Head, and other times they would be over Wai'alae Drive-In, but whichever way, they would be getting way out there. Then we would watch and wait.

I wonder, did Israel feel like he too was sailing away on the winds like his kite?

Kaimuki has always had a tight-knit community and "small-town" feeling. This photo taken from the Kaimuki fire station follows the neighborhood all the way up into Palolo Valley. [Bishop Museum]

As soon as it happened, SNAP, Israel would bellow, *"Buckaloose!!!"* The whole park would hear. Naturally, I would follow with a howl, *"Hawhooo!!"* Of course, when one goes, SNAP, SNAP, the others will follow. And I swear, we would just stand there for minutes and watch the kites as they just kept on sailing away. They'd fly past Diamond Head, out of sight and out to sea. Or just keep climbing the Koʻolaus, seeming like they'd keep on going, so free. I wonder, did Israel feel like he too was sailing away on the winds like his kite? Maybe that's why he only flew each kite once. With the kite flying so free…how sad it would be to have to return it to ground.

Friends and Neighbors

We had to be careful playing around in the neighborhood. Not that we'd be getting into trouble, though that happened, but because someone would always end up feeding you. If not one of our parents, my next door "Hawaiian Grandma and Grandpa" would. What a blessing to have had Grandma and Grandpa AhNee taking care of us. Babysitting us when sick, letting us play in their courtyard, having an open door to us anytime.

In fact, one day, Grandma took me into the kitchen and showed me where everything was. She pointed out the snacks on the counter, the juice in the fridge, cups by the sink. She said, "Anytime you want something, you know where stay. You know how to come inside if we not home, and when pau, put in sink." I'll never forget her next words. She said, "No matter what, NO BOTHER Grandpa. Get yourself." And that is exactly how we did things. Wow, never mind having open doors, we had open refrigerators. And I swear, I never bothered Grandpa.

You know, Grandpa never really said a whole lot to us, not like Grandma, but he was always watching us making sure we were all right. He'd be working on something as if oblivious to us, but he'd have Grandma make us lunch or something, so apparently we weren't that oblivious to him. I guess that was just his style. Grandma, on the other hand, would make sure you gave her a hug and kiss, and all that. You can imagine. Oh, how dear and precious they were…

Buckaloose

One day, a few of us were playing on the street in front of our homes. There was a telephone pole right in front of my house, and the electrical wire went from that telephone pole to the house across the street. So with a tennis ball, we would stand in two teams, throw the ball over the line, and the team on the other side would catch it. The key was to make sure the ball went over the wire, and not to hit the wire! And of course, the higher you threw the ball, the better.

Israel was on my side, I know because I remember him yelling. Someone had thrown the ball too far, and I was the one who took off trying to catch it. But as I was chasing it…along came a car. Apparently this car had made a turn from Harding onto 20th Ave, and we were on a collision course. Fortunately, the car stopped...but I didn't. In fact, I didn't even know the car was there. I did hear Israel scream out something, but I just thought he was cheering me on as I was about to make a spectacular over-the-shoulder catch. There I was, full stride, arms stretched forward, the symbol of grace, then BOOM! My legs hit the front grill, stopping me in my tracks—but with my upper body still going forward. I slammed chest, arms, and head into the hood. As I looked up, I saw two faces leaning forward, four big bug eyes, and two dropped jaws. Then at that split second, WHAM! The tennis ball slammed into the windshield, the two heads flew back hard, they didn't know what hit them!

I really didn't know what to do, so I just ran home and hid behind the bushes. The car drove off down the street, and as soon as it passed, everybody was just cracking up, rolling on the ground. I stepped out and all they could do was point at me, and kept on laughing…no one even asked me if I was all right.

I guess we did a lot of running back in those days, even in school. One time in our 4th grade P.E. class we were playing football, and, of course, Israel was on my team. We figured that even though there were a gazillion kids on the field, we would hand the ball off to Israel, and just let him run over everybody. Maybe help a little by pushing from the rear, but basically just run over everybody. Well, on that first play, I handed the ball off to Israel, and as soon as he hit the scrimmage line, he literally ran into a wall…a wall of kids. There were so many bodies, Israel wasn't about to go anywhere. But the funny part was that they couldn't get him down! He was just standing there with a mountain of kids piled on, really being held upright from everyone pushing and pulling from all sides. Nowhere to go, not even enough room to fall down.

On the next play we figured we'd send all the big boys to lead Israel through the line, open a hole or something to get by. For some reason, it seemed like it would work. There was a huge hole in the line, Israel was picking up speed, and as soon as he hit the hole, BOOM! A whole wall of kids popped up from somewhere, don't know where, but that hole closed and kids started piling on again. He still wouldn't go down. I was actually amazed. He was carrying some weight with everyone hanging on, and he still wouldn't go down. We kept playing, trying new strategies every time. But pretty soon, I heard someone utter, "Where's Israel?" I turned and saw he was sitting on the side, up against the fence. Someone asked what he was doing, and I took the liberty of answering, "Just tired." You know what happened? A few of us quit the game, walked over to Israel, sat down and kept him company. The teacher knew he was tired, and didn't make us leave him to himself, kind of cool of her. That's what's nice about friends, it really never mattered what you were doing, just as long as you did it together.

There was at least one game we enjoyed that didn't require a lot of running—Sky Inning. For those of you who are not sure how to play, it's a simple game. You have a batter who hits the ball out to those waiting in the field. If the ball is caught by someone, that person becomes the batter. If not, the batter might allow some handicap for the fielder to advance closer, by allowing him to toss the ball up, running, and catching the ball. The batter lays the bat down and the fielder rolls the ball to hit the bat. If the ball hits the bat and you catch the ball before it hits the ground, you keep batting. If you drop the ball, you switch with the fielder. Anyway, we used to play this down Israel's lane. It was perfect as long as you hit kind of straight.

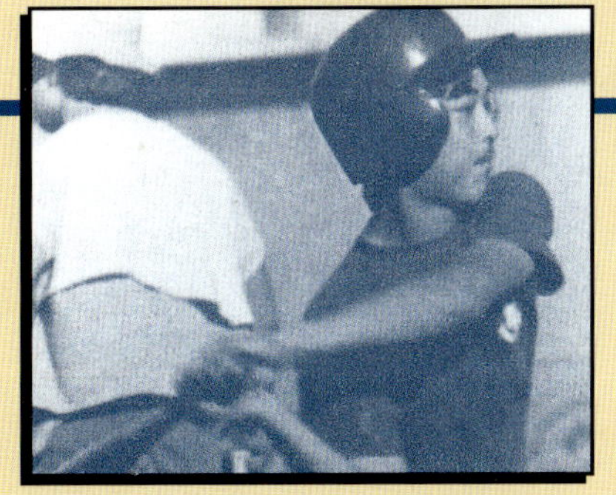

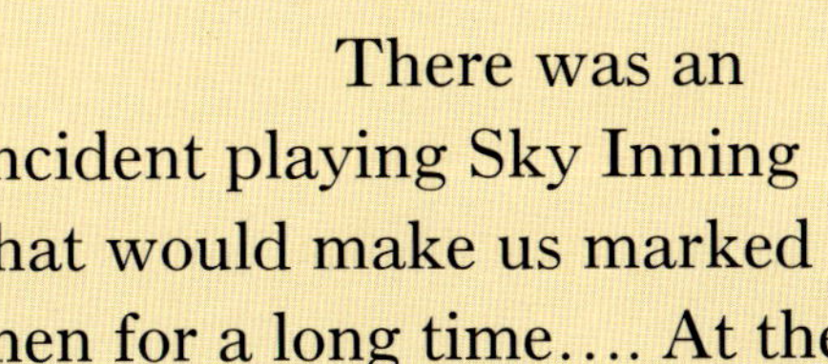

There was an incident playing Sky Inning that would make us marked men for a long time…. At the beginning of his lane, there was this house with a driveway that opened onto the lane. As we were playing, the ball got by me and rolled into the yard. I figured it was no big deal and was just going to run in and get it. So just as I was about to run after the ball, "she" came out with the ball in her hand. "She" being the lady of the house. At first I thought she came out to say hi and give us back our ball, I was so naïve. By this time Israel had also come up, and we were trying to listen to what she was saying. She was actually giving us directions to Petrie Park! I looked over at Israel and he looked at me, and we didn't catch the hint! Not at all. And this lady got madder. She just turned around and walked away. Israel and I just stood there silent, looking at each other thinking, "she took our ball!" For me, I was shocked. I wasn't used to this kind of neighbor. And this was just the beginning.

For a while there, she kept an eye on us pretty good, with a few scoldings in between. We couldn't figure out why she had the same kind of schedule as us, and I think she waited in her yard just so she could make sure we didn't hang around her house playing. When I used to walk up to Israel's place, I would see her and be as nice as I could be, but I think that only irritated her more.

Playing for Keeps

Back in the old days we played marbles. We had all kinds of marbles. From the cat's eye, to the bumbuchas, all the way down to the little peewees. My favorite was this three-quarter orange and white swirl, made just for my fingers. Marbles were so popular that a teacher had a fish tank made just for them! Anytime a marble dropped to the floor in class, it got donated to the fish tank. I dropped a bag of marbles once... and the fish tank looked great!

As for Israel, he played for keeps. Well, kind of. He had this little tiny blue-green peewee marble. It was too tiny to shoot with, so he only used it when he was in trouble and about to get hit. Otherwise he'd use a big bumbucha, figuring it's so big he cannot miss. Well one day, I got his tiny little blue-green peewee! He was shocked, and I was too. But he wouldn't give it up. Instead he gave me his bumbucha, saying we're playing for the marble we were shooting with. Back then you didn't get mad and fight, saying "you owe me" or anything like that. We just laughed. This big guy who cherished a tiny marble, how can you take that away? And how in the world did he not lose that peewee? Ahhh, he had a secret place for that marble, and if I'm not mistaken, it was in his pants cuff. Worked for him.

I really don't remember a whole lot that we did in the classroom. Mostly just what happened in P.E. and during recess. In fact, I don't remember if Israel was in my 5th grade class with Miss Shima or not. Ooh, Miss Shima, wherever you are out there, THANK YOU. I'll never forget you. And I also remember Miss Medeiros' music class. Israel definitely had an edge there when trying to learn the ukulele. Everyone wanted to sit next to him so they could cheat and follow his fingers. But whether he was in my class after, or not, didn't matter. The damage was already done.

Back then you didn't get mad and fight, saying "you owe me" or anything like that. We just laughed.

Miss Shima's 5th grade students at Wai'alae Elementary School smile for the camera. Remember the days when shoes were optional at school?

Sometime at the end of 6th grade, Israel's family moved to Palolo. But we knew we were still going to see him at Kaimuki Intermediate! After he did move, it just so happened I still kind of got to see him after school, for a moment. His dad used to pick him and Skippy up from school. Skippy was older and already at Kaimuki Intermediate, so each day, they would be riding up Pahoa Avenue in their station wagon, heading home. Now it's important to understand, between 22nd Avenue to 20th Avenue, Pahoa Avenue is a steep hill. And since their station wagon was kind of bust up, they would make their way up kind of slowly…and real low to the ground. I'd be standing on the wall of Petrie Park as they passed by, waving shaka. Skippy would be in the front passenger seat, and he'd give me that head bob, saying "Howzit." Israel would be in the back passenger seat, but he wouldn't even look my way! Oh yes, he'd be sitting back there, looking forward, head held high, nose kind of in the air, like some majestic king touring his countryside. But his right hand would be out, pointing downward, giving me the shaka sign. I would just laugh and admire his classic pose.

Anyway, elementary school would of course feel like a dream as we then started to prepare for our next step: the Teenage years.

Kaimuki Intermediate

Now, if you were to walk from the office at Kaimuki Intermediate School to the cafeteria, you would pass a landing area. On this landing there was a bench, affectionately known as Israel's Bench. It was there that we spent some special moments. I guess like everybody else, when I got to Kaimuki Intermediate, I just gravitated toward friendly, familiar faces, and Israel was a friendly face. We used to meet before school, and start our day from there.

For me, walking to school was quick, only four blocks away. But since Israel had moved to Palolo, he rode the bus to school. He actually came in with some guys we didn't know, but of course, we soon became friends. One of those first mornings, the guys were introducing one another. Someone pointed to me and said, "That's Sam." But all of a sudden Israel said, "NO!" Kind of loudly, I might add. Then he goes, "He's King Kong!" Those that didn't know me cracked up, but as far as Israel was concerned, that was my name. Honest.

Before and after school, the outdoor benches at Kaimuki Intermediate were the place to hang out and talk story with friends.

During this time, one's loyalty was tested as you met new friends while still trying to keep the old.

Something else happened during those first days. We met at the bench as usual, but this time they had some food. They had bought it in Kaimuki town before they came to school. Now before I continue, I want to tell you something about Israel. We really enjoyed the food at Woolworths, and he really liked the manapua from the old Chinese man that used to walk down the streets. Remember him? Carrying a pole on his shoulders, with a huge metal container on each end that looked like a trash can, but they came apart in layers. Each layer had something different, from manapua to pork hash, pepeau, half moon...He would be walking down the street yelling, "Yohoooo!" I always ran to Israel's house to get him when the manapua man came by. Anyway, even more than the dim-sum, he used to love the corned beef hash at the Okazu-ya right across 9th Avenue Bakery in Kaimuki town. Hands down, I don't care what anyone says, his favorite was the hash! For that hash...you wouldn't believe.

One morning, with everybody just grinding, Israel invited me to meet him in the morning in Kaimuki town. Now I really wasn't too keen about walking ten blocks uphill to town, and I usually ate at home in the morning anyway. So I kept saying "No." Then you should have seen this. He pulled out this whole piece of hash, handling it like precious fine crystal, and offered the whole thing to me. He was thinking if I ate it, I'd be hooked. You should know, I'm not too thrilled about hash. So I politely turned him down. Then he carefully broke it in half, handing me one piece. Now I had to take it. How could I refuse? I must admit, though, it tasted good. But still, I started thinking I better meet him in Kaimuki town after all, at least that way I'll be able to get what I want to eat. So that was the start of our Intermediate years.

It was actually quite an eye-opener for me. Kids were coming from Ainakoa, up to Kaimuki town to transfer to the Ruger bus, then on to school. So there were quite a bit of us in town in the morning. I didn't go every morning, but a few times each week was the norm. Sometimes I even took the 9th Avenue overpass and caught the bus up to town. It was only ten cents, and with the transfer, it didn't matter anyway. Wow, this was when we still had Ben Franklin, Kaimuki Theatre, Thrifty's, Hon Kung restaurant ... and Dick's Danish Pastry Shoppe, my personal favorite. I believe our favorite crack seed store is still there today, and that's the name, Crack Seed Store, easy for us to remember. Right on Kokohead Avenue, across from the bus stop. And, oh yes, there was Kaimuki Bowl ... some good memories there.

I believe our favorite crack seed store is still there today, and that's the name, Crack Seed Store, easy for us to remember.

The Crack Seed Store on Koko Head Avenue still offers a variety of treats.

One day, it was already time to leave and catch the bus from Kaimuki town to school, but Israel was late. As I was ready to leave, Israel showed up, getting off the bus from lower Kaimuki, with ukulele and bus transfer in hand. We met and he said he wanted to go to the Okazu-ya across the street next to Thrifty's. Actually he said, "We go kaukau." But I knew what he meant. I also figured we were going to be late already, so why not? But that Okazu-ya didn't have hash. So guess what? The smart kids went to school. As for me and Israel, we walked down to 9th Avenue, got the hash, and walked back up to our bus stop. And since we didn't walk too fast, we were very late for school. But we were willing to be late for a piece of hash…such are priorities in life. Well, actually, Israel was willing to be late, I could have done without the hash.

Funny, not once did anyone come with me to Dick's Danish Pastry Shoppe, or 9th Avenue Bakery. They would always go for the bento food. Maybe they went on other days when I wasn't there. With Israel, it was always community food anyway. We just had to watch what we ate first. Sometimes the flavors wouldn't seem like they would compliment each other. Chocolate éclair and shoyu hot dogs? It worked for us.

I believe it was at our first school assembly that we found out why Israel's neighbor had a similar schedule. It turned out she was the head cafeteria lady, and we were told that we had to do cafeteria duty someday. Oh boy. Soon after that, if not that very day, I saw Israel sitting under the tree after school, not looking too happy. Since school had just gotten out, several of us started to gather under the tree. It was noisy, just people talking. Then Israel looked up and said, "I no like mash potatoes." And I caught on immediately. Apparently no one else got it because they were going off on saying how much they liked mashed potatoes, and how often they got to eat them, and so on. But Israel was just sitting there shaking his head. Then I opened my mouth and told Israel, "Never mind mashing potatoes, you going have to peel 'em first!" Then we started cracking up. No one knew what we were talking about.

We went off on each other. "Israel, you going have to wake up super early for start peeling those potatoes." "Then you can mash 'em." "King Kong, they going hang you by the ankles for go inside and scrub the big pots!" And we kept going back and forth, making up the worst for each other, just cracking up. We were laughing so hard it hurt. Israel was saying, "No make, no make!" between gasps. Then all of a sudden, when we got to the part about the slop, for some reason, we weren't laughing anymore. Israel's last comment was, "She going get us." And I believed him.

Fortunately we didn't have to face her that year, and as time went on, I hoped she'd forget who I was, and not even recognize me anymore. So 7th grade went on smoothly, without us realizing that we were changing. What can I say… girls! Wow, I was so naïve, I didn't know what to do with them. All I knew was that they were so pretty. During this time, one's loyalty was tested as you met new friends while still trying to keep the old. We were very fortunate that we had Israel's bench to meet at. It was the one stable part of our changing days. Even as we were running around, sometime going our separate ways, we still had Israel's bench to return to.

By the time summer came along, things had changed. After class, it was now fun to get together with new friends, and we went all over the place. Kahala Beach, Diamond Head, Kahala Mall…what a terrific summer. But then, there was also the realization that there was no such thing as "Summer Fun" anymore. Now it was "Summer School," our bodies and minds were growing up. Those were probably some of the most exciting, and yet, saddest times of our lives…when innocence started passing us by. It was a lot easier when we were sheltered from the world.

Cruising Waikiki

When we got back together in our 8th grade year, Israel spoke a lot about how he went down and spent his days in Waikiki over the summer. Now, he was excited about Kahala Mall years before, so you can imagine his excitement over Waikiki! He kept bugging me to go with him, but I was just not that adventurous—in fact, I was chicken—so I really hesitated in going. But Israel wasn't to be denied.

One morning when I met him in town, we caught the bus to school as usual. But this time I just so happened to sit right behind him, towards the back of the bus. When the bus got to the first Kaimuki Intermediate bus stop, he stood up, let some people pass, except me, and just stood there. The bus started going again, and I thought we'd get off at the next stop. It was actually closer to the portables where our classes were, so I thought that was a good idea. But at the next stop, he just stood there, not letting me get by, blocking the aisle. I didn't say anything and

Cutting class to catch the bus down to Waikiki was a grand adventure: International Marketplace, Fun Factory, and Kalakaua Avenue abuzz with action! [Lawrence Hata/Bishop Museum]

...you can imagine his excitement over Waikiki!

Zippy's Kapahulu was a good place to stop off for a quick bowl of chili and rice. [FCH Enterprises, Inc.]

just stood there. Now this time, all the students got off, except us. Finally as we were going past Diamond Head, he turned to me, smiled, and said, "Waikiki." I didn't know what to say, I was too busy thinking how much trouble I'd be in for cutting class! This was the first time I ever did anything like this, and it was all Israel's fault! But I was cool…well, as cool as one can look with an arm full of schoolbooks, walking around Waikiki.

Now for some reason, we got to Waikiki in a heartbeat. Getting to Kapahulu was really quick since we were already on the bus and didn't have to wait for one. And as soon as we got to the Kapahulu bus stop, the bus came and the next thing we knew, we were already in Waikiki. BUT, do you know what's happening in Waikiki at 8:30 a.m.? Nothing! International Marketplace was closed, Fun Factory, closed. What a waste...well, it was worth the experience. So we headed back to school, stopping off at Zippy's Kapahulu on the way back.

Now Israel knew I wasn't going to Waikiki with him so early, so the next time, he waited until recess. And yes, I went. We took off at mid-morning and he said we would be back at lunch. I believed him. Now this time, Israel was very pleased to show me around, and we had a great day. But as you know, time can get away from you. So when we got back to school, the moment our feet hit the campus, a school bell rang. In a moment we realized which bell it was, and Israel said, "Pau school." I didn't know what to do, neither did Israel, so he said, "We go back." And we did. We rode the now crowded bus back to Waikiki. This wasn't the last time either.

One time we got off the bus at Kapahulu Library and walked around the Ala Wai for fun. I remember he said that there should be a waterfall at the beginning of the Ala Wai, near the library. It was just something he wanted to see happen back then. Just thought I'd pass that on.

Kapahulu Library on the Ala Wai Canal.

Silence is Golden

It turned out that I was the first to do cafeteria duty. I didn't think it was all that bad, but Israel sure thought my story was hilarious, so I'll tell you what I told him. Just before lunch, a bunch of us kids reported to the cafeteria, and waited behind the counter for instructions. I was checking out those large pots, and I could picture myself hanging upside down cleaning them. I think I could have fit.

Now the head cafeteria lady, our friend, whom I hoped had forgotten me, came out and the first thing she said was, "SILENCE…IS…GOLDEN." Then to make sure, she repeated herself, "SILENCE IS GOLDEN. Good. I'm going to assign to you your positions and explain to you what you need to do. First," she pointed to a couple of guys, "you're going to be line monitors. You stand near the entrance and make sure no one cuts in line. Make sure they come in in an orderly way. Got that?" They nodded. Then she turned to the rest of us and started to split us up to work the service line. I thought this was going to be O.K., she was too busy to pay attention to little ‘ol me.

Then just at that moment, she turned to me and said ominously, “King Kong, you follow me.” I could tell by the way everybody just froze that they were a little shocked too. After all, how many elders would call a kid by the name “King Kong?” Anyway, she went on to say, “You stay three steps behind me and follow me wherever I go, understand?” I nodded. She continued, “You just do as I tell you, O.K.?” Again I nodded. Just to let you know, Israel got a kick when I told him I had to follow three steps behind her. I didn’t think it was that funny.

So, as soon as the first bell rang, I followed the head cafeteria lady out into the cafeteria and watched as the students filed in. The first thing I noticed was the noise! It was super quiet just a moment ago, but now there was noise everywhere. I didn’t realize how loud it could get. And as I watched the students file in, the head cafeteria lady started talking to some other worker. At that moment a friend saw me, waved and said “Howzit.” So I just made a small shaka sign and just mouthed the word “Howzit.” No sense in trying to speak too loud over all this noise. But as soon as I did that, the head cafeteria lady turned on me and said, “SILENCE…IS…GOLDEN!!!” Gee, with all that noise and her talking to somebody else, how could she have heard me say anything? But she did. So I didn’t wave or say “Hi” to anyone else. I couldn’t figure out what to do, so I just stood there and watched the students keep on filing in. But in that split second, the head cafeteria lady had walked away! And I had no idea which way she went. Aaargh. When I told Israel this last part, he was rolling on the ground, laughing, he knew I was in trouble now. It just so happened, I saw her standing behind the service line, and I was making my way fast hoping that she hadn’t missed me yet. She had her back to me and I was sneaking up fast, but as soon as I got there, without her looking at me, she says, “Three steps. You know how much is three steps?” I was just about to say “No, how MANY?” but I was saved by a shortage of milk. Before I could continue, we had to get more milk from the refrigerator for the serving line, immediately. YES! I was so happy to be working!

Somehow I got through cafeteria duty without being sent to the counselor, so that was good. But could you imagine what would have happened if there hadn’t been a shortage of milk at that moment? I might still be on cafeteria duty. Well, Israel had a blast when I told him my story, he was laughing, teasing me. Then I said, “You next.” He stopped laughing.

One of the happiest times I ever saw Israel came when he WAS next. One day not long afterward, as the lunch bell went off for my class, I headed for the cafeteria. I started across the grass courtyard and saw Israel standing on the walkway, holding his ukulele. There were a bunch of guys hanging around, talking story. As soon as Israel saw me, he just started smiling and giggling, rocking back and forth, strumming his uke. As I got closer, he became even happier. By the time I reached him, his happiness was having that contagious effect. I started to laugh, and I didn't even know what was going on yet. So I asked, "Howzit?" He answered with, "I stay on cafeteria duty!" I had to stop, think, and ask, "What, how come you out here then?" He said, "I stay line monitor!" And by then Israel was laughing so hard, rocking back and forth, that I started to laugh, but I still didn't know what was so funny yet. So I asked, "How come you not at the front?" And now Israel straightened up a little and said, "I told the buggas for behave!" That's it. I realized the importance of his words, and we were both just rolling…See, all he had done was walk out of the cafeteria, say, "You buggas behave!" and kept on walking. That was his cafeteria duty! You know at that moment, it was like life was coming full circle, and we passed the test. From the day she took our ball, to finding out who she was, to "You buggas behave!" *Life really came full circle…*

Breaking Free

T*owards the end of 8th grade,* I was seeing less and less of Israel, and a lot more of, what else? Girls. Sorry, I guess I'm just simple-minded. But by now, meeting Israel in town was really hit or miss. Sometimes Israel wouldn't show up for breakfast or for school. So he would have to show up in school and make me promise to meet him the next morning. That wasn't guaranteed either, but there was still Israel's bench. Around this time, he'd stay there a little longer than he should. See, I'd go to class and come back at next recess to find Israel still at his bench... Yeah, he missed class. But to me, not all seemed lost. Israel was already playing for Makaha Sons of Ni'ihau, and I was proud of him. Hey, he would even play for us. Free, private concert, compliments of Israel. So even as we were going through some growing pains, there was no doubt we'd make it. It seemed that all would turn out well.

Towards the end of 8th grade, school was about one thing only: GIRLS.

So even as we were going through some growing pains, there was no doubt we'd make it.

By the time 9th grade came around, I don't think I ever went to meet Israel in Kaimuki town, and Waikiki was no longer an attraction to me. Oh wait, there was another time. I did meet Israel in town. Guess what happened? Yes, we ate hash! But when we rode the bus to Kaimuki Intermediate, Israel didn't get off. I presume he continued on his way to Waikiki. Though I wonder, because he had wanted me to check out Ala Moana too! You know Israel. The hard part for me was that Israel was hardly ever in school anymore, not even at his bench.

From the 1977 *"Kā hea o Keale"* album cover, photographed by Elizabeth and George Studios. [Tropical Music, Inc.]

The last time I saw Israel at Kaimuki Intermediate was on a day after December 5th, but before Christmas. I had just started dating this girl on December 5th. And soon after, as we were walking down the hall holding hands together, we saw Israel at his bench. He called out, and we waved shaka to each other. My girlfriend even asked me if I knew Israel…I said, "Yeah."

A very short time later I had to run an errand to the school office. But as I was returning to class, I saw Israel sitting at his bench, so I walked over. He smiled, but he looked serious at the same time. He said, “Sam, I’m so proud of you.” I said thanks and we talked about my girlfriend and how we met. But my mind was reeling…he called me Sam. And he was proud? What was going on?

Then he said, “I going drop out.” I just looked at him and said, “How come?” His answer was simple, “No sense.” And I knew what he meant. We talked a bit, starting with our hanabatta days, to the changes we were going through, and what might happen. That’s why he was so proud of me. It was like I was ready to move on with my life, while he didn’t seem too sure of his. As we continued to talk, we both realized we were saying our goodbyes. Our hearts were heavy, and yet hopeful. I wished him the best, and started to walk away. When I was a part way off, Israel called out, “Hey, King Kong…BUCKALOOSE!!!” I echoed with, “Hawhooooo!!!” then slowly made my way back to class.

The End

Buckaloose

From the cover of the 1999 Makaha Sons of Ni'ihau CD, *Nā Mele Henoheno, Nā Makahiki Mua, helu 'ekahi,* photograph taken by Jacqueline Skylark Rossetti (circa 1976). [Tropical Music, Inc.]

They'd fly past Diamond Head, out of sight and out to sea. Or just keep climbing the Ko'olaus, seeming like they'd keep on going, so free.

EPILOGUE

I would never get another chance to really sit and talk with Israel, even though we did meet at times at Kalani High School. So, after Kalani High School I went into the Air Force and was basically missing from Hawai‘i. And by the time I returned, Israel was now Bruddah Iz, and as for me, I just kept on trying to get by in life. I guess, just like each one of us living here in Paradise.

Many stories were almost long forgotten. If it wasn't for my brother and some friends, I wouldn't have remembered many things, even going to Kahala Mall. And since we were young, we never got into any philosophical discussions. It was more like, "What we going do next?" In fact, not until we said our goodbyes did we ever talk seriously. How strange. You know some things are happening, but you never really talk about them. I'm not even sure, but I believe his dad passed away when we were in 7th grade at Kaimuki Intermediate, we just didn't talk about it. I never met his mom, and of course, I never asked. I guess that's just the way of the local boy, communicating without words. Heck, that's why we got pidgin. The least amount of words, the better. And Israel was a Master. He'd say one or two words, and you'd have to fill in the rest. See, pidgin makes you listen with your heart, not your ears. Otherwise, you'd miss the message. I thank God, He allowed me to have such a friend, such a childhood. Even with the head cafeteria lady. It was just fun messing around.

I heard that Israel came to know Jesus Christ. If that is true, then there is a place prepared for him, and in that place, I believe, that there is a bench... Well, Israel, you save a seat for me. Let me introduce you to my family, my wife June, my son Dustin, and my daughter Courtney. You'd be so proud of me. Dustin has a few questions for you, he doesn't believe we played Chase Master together. But he's already practicing his ukulele, even playing some of your songs, maybe you two can jam. He going call you Uncle Israel, and I think you'd like him, he's just like me. Baby King Kong! Just teasing. So anyway my friend, till that day...

"Buckaloose!"